MEXICO'S
NORTHERN STATES

Chihuahua, Coahuila, Durango, Nuevo León,

San Luis Potosí, Tamaulipas, and Zacatecas

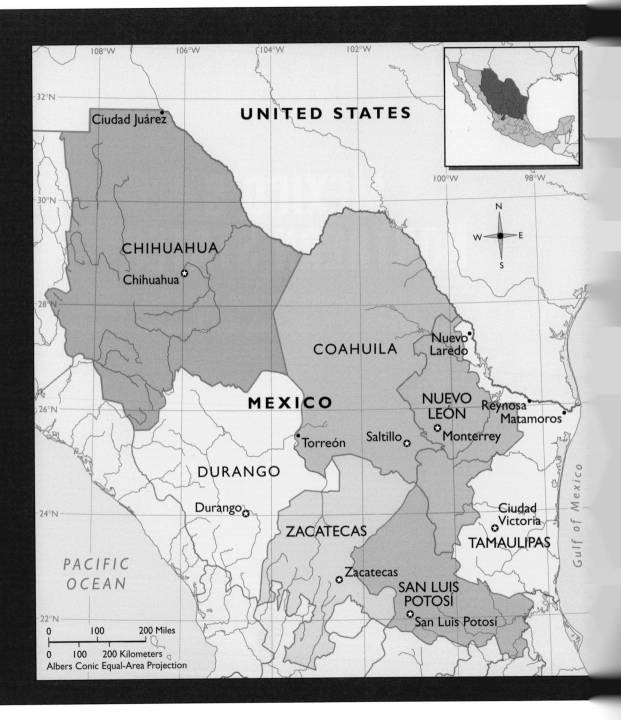

108°W   106°W   104°W   102°W

32°N

Ciudad Juárez

UNITED STATES

100°W   98°W

30°N

CHIHUAHUA

Chihuahua

28°N

COAHUILA

N
W   E
S

Nuevo
Laredo

26°N

MEXICO

NUEVO
LEÓN

Reynosa
Matamoros

Torreón

Saltillo   Monterrey

DURANGO

Durango

Ciudad
Victoria

ZACATECAS

TAMAULIPAS

Gulf of Mexico

PACIFIC
OCEAN

24°N

22°N

Zacatecas

SAN LUIS
POTOSÍ

San Luis Potosí

0   100   200 Miles

0   100   200 Kilometers

Albers Conic Equal-Area Projection

MEXICO
Leading the Southern Hemisphere

MEXICO'S NORTHERN STATES

Chihuahua, Coahuila, Durango, Nuevo León,
San Luis Potosí, Tamaulipas, and Zacatecas

MASON CREST
PHILADELPHIA

Mason Crest
450 Parkway Drive, Suite D
Broomall, PA 19008
www.masoncrest.com

©2015 by Mason Crest, an imprint of National Highlights, Inc.

Printed and bound in the United States of America.

CPSIA Compliance Information: Batch #M2014.
For further information, contact Mason Crest at 1-866-MCP-Book.

First printing

1 3 5 7 9 8 6 4 2

Library of Congress Cataloging-in-Publication Data
on file at the Library of Congress

ISBN: 978-1-4222-3227-9 (hc)
ISBN: 978-1-4222-8692-0 (ebook)

Mexico: Leading the Southern Hemisphere series ISBN: 978-1-4222-3213-2

TABLE OF CONTENTS

MEXICO
Leading the Southern Hemisphere

KEY ICONS TO LOOK FOR:

 Text-dependent questions: These questions send the reader back to the text for more careful attention to the evidence presented there.

 Words to understand: These words with their easy-to-understand definitions will increase the reader's understanding of the text, while building vocabulary skills.

 Series glossary of key terms: This back-of-the book glossary contains terminology used throughout this series. Words found here increase the reader's ability to read and comprehend higher-level books and articles in this field.

 Research projects: Readers are pointed toward areas of further inquiry connected to each chapter. Suggestions are provided for projects that encourage deeper research and analysis.

 Sidebars: This boxed material within the main text allows readers to build knowledge, gain insights, explore possibilities, and broaden their perspectives by weaving together additional information to provide realistic and holistic perspectives.

TIMELINE

150 B.C.	Teotihuacán is built.
A.D. 750	Teotihuacán is abandoned.
300–900	Peak cultural growth of the Maya.
	Aztecs begin to conquer other tribes for control of Mexico.
1325	Aztecs build Tenochtitlán.
1521	Spanish take control of Mexico.
1810	Father Miguel Hidalgo calls for Mexico's independence from Spain.
1821	Mexico wins its independence.
1862	France invades Mexico.
1867	Benito Juárez triumphs over the French, executes the Emperor Maximilian, and resumes his presidency.
1876	Porfirio Díaz begins his period of dictatorship.
1910–1921	The Mexican Revolution.
1968	Mexico hosts the Summer Olympic Games, and violence breaks out during a student protest.
2000	Vicente Fox becomes president.
2004	Monterrey hosts the Summit of the Americas, in which the leaders of 34 Western Hemisphere democracies meet to discuss political issues.
2006	65 workers are killed in an explosion at a Coahuila coal mine; Felipe Calderón is elected president of Mexico.
2008	Despite the efforts of Mexican law enforcement agencies, drug-related gang violence remains a major problem in the northern states near the U.S. border as drug cartels fight for control over smuggling routes.

8

2009 The Mexican government reports that more than 6,500 people were killed in drug-related incidents during the year, making it the deadliest year of the narco conflict since it was escalated by President Calderón. Ciudad Juárez finishes the year with the highest reported murder rate in the world.

2012 Enrique Peña Nieto is elected president of Mexico, receiving 38 percent of the vote. His election returns the PRI to power after 12 years of PAN rule. He is sworn in as president on December 1.

2013 Monterrey, CF wins the CONCACAF Champions Cup for an unprecedented third straight time.

2014 Joaquin "El Chapo" Guzman, leader of the powerful Sinaloa drug cartel, is arrested by the Mexican military, with the assistance of U.S. authorities.

View of the mountain Cerro de la Silla, from a plaza in Monterrey.

WORDS TO UNDERSTAND

irrigated—brought water to the land by artificial means.

migrate—to move from one region to another.

plateau—high, level land.

For more than 1,000 miles (1,600 km) the Río Grande marks the northern border of Mexico. Here, the river flows between the Mexican state of Coahuila and the U.S. state of Texas.

THE LAND

Imagine Mexico as a giant letter "vee" with its the top opening toward the United States. Two rugged mountain ranges form the edges of the vee—the "Mother" mountains: the Sierra Madre Oriental and the Sierra Madre Occidental. In the north, they are wide apart, separated by the *Meseta Central* (the Central **Plateau**). The northern states of Mexico lie within the top of this vee. This region is composed of seven states: Chihuahua, Coahuila, Durango, Nuevo León, San Luis Potosí, Tamaulipas, and Zacatecas.

When you look at a map of Mexico it is difficult to tell which areas are *tierra caliente, tierra templada,* or *tierra fría*—the hot-, medium-, and cold-weather areas. This is because the climate in Mexico is determined not by whether the land is in the north or the south as much as by elevation—the higher up in the mountains, the cooler the region. Much of this area falls into the medium-weather or temperate zone. The state of Tamaulipas, which lies along the Gulf Coast, however, is *tierra caliente,* as is the northernmost part of the land that slopes down toward the Río Grande.

The northern edge of this area lies along the Río Grande, the river that marks about 1,000 miles (1,600 km) of the border between Mexico and the

United States. The Río Grande, called the Río Bravo by the Mexicans, is a shallow winding river that empties into the Gulf of Mexico. It brings together rivers from all along the eastern side of Mexico.

The Chihuahua Desert lies just south of the Río Grande. In the native language, Chihuahua means "dry, sandy land," and the Chihuahua is the largest desert in North America. This desert covers about 175,000 square miles and is bigger than the entire state of California. It is called a "rain shadow desert," because the two mountain ranges on either side of it stop the moist air from the Gulf of Mexico and the Pacific Ocean from reaching the middle area. Unlike many deserts, the Chihuahua is not flat. There are many small mountain ranges running through it, and within the cracks between mountains are river basins. The differences in altitude mean that the Chihuahua is home to more kinds of wildlife than most other deserts.

The Indians who once inhabited this area could not farm but lived by hunting and gathering, sometimes eating the cactus or even iguanas and insects. There are 500 different kinds of cactus in Mexico, and Indians once used some of them for food and drink. The dry land cannot support much life unless it is *irrigated*.

Deep canyons cut through this rough scenery. The flat area, called "Meseta Central"—the central plateau—is cradled between the two jagged mountain ranges. The land sloping toward the Río Grande has become a region of large cities with skyscrapers and factories. It is also a land where there are still Indians living in caves. Orchards and croplands flourish in fertile valleys reclaimed by irrigation.

The area known as Copper Canyon is twice the size of the Grand Canyon in Arizona. Copper Canyon is not a single canyon but the union of several deep,

Copper Canyon is the name for a group of six canyons in the Sierra Madre range of southwestern Chihuahua.

spectacular canyons. It is cut by the Urique River and has deep, wide gorges so remote that parts of it have never been explored on foot. This region is also known as the Sierra Tarahumara, after the Indians who live there. No copper is found here; the canyon is named for the color of its walls.

The Sierra Madre Occidental forms the western rim of the Plateau of Mexico, and it runs from Chihuahua down through Durango and then into Zacatecas, the Mexican states that lie to the south. For hundreds of years, this mountain range

4

The Chihuahua Desert stretches across several Mexican states, as well as across the border and into the United States. This fishhook barrel cactus thrives in Nuevo León.

blocked transportation between the plateau and the west coast, forming a natural barrier. Paved roads and a railroad were not built across it until the 1900s.

This range includes some of Mexico's most rugged land. Short, steep streams flowing to the Pacific Ocean have cut canyons more than a mile (1.6 kilometers) deep through the mountains.

Higher in the mountains, the weather gets colder. Here bear and sheep live. In the winter the forests at the tops of the mountains may be covered in snow, while the valleys beneath are still tropically warm. These western mountains climb to the height of 9,200 feet. The Tarahumara Indians *migrate* from the caves where they live in the summer, down to the warmer areas when frigid winter winds arrive. The state of Durango is also famous for its huge desert scorpions.

The Sierra Madre Oriental, the plateau's eastern rim, runs through the states of Coahuila and Nuevo León. These mountains are actually a series of

The Cascade of Minas Viejas is located in San Luis Potosí. The two waterfalls are approximately 165 feet (50 m) high.

ranges. In many places, between the ranges, highways and railroads climb up to the plateau from the east coast. Though the Sierra Madre Oriental is not a region with fertile farmland, this area is rich in metals such as silver, gold, lead, iron, and zinc.

In Tamaulipas, beside the Gulf of Mexico, the land is flat and low with marshes and lagoons, alligators and crocodiles. This is *tierra caliente* or hot land. Tamaulipas borders the United States on the north, Veracruz and San Luis Potosí to the south, Veracruz and the Gulf of Mexico to the east. In the native people's language, the name may mean "High Mountains," "Tribe of Olives," or "Place of Much Prayer." In the north, Tamaulipas is fairly dry and warm with only a little rain. In the south and southeast it is warmer and wetter. In the mountains, the climate ranges from warm to temperate according to altitude.

There are places in Tamaulipas so remote that the people who live there don't use money. Many of these live in a protected region called the El Cielo biosphere reserve. This is an area where all the wildlife and plants are protected from harm.

The Huasteca is the region of the Sierra Madre Oriental that covers the south of Tamaulipas as well as the northern region of San Luis Potosí (and Veracruz). It rains there between 60 and 150 inches annually. Much of the Huasteca is covered with tropical cloud forests. Here you can find spectacular waterfalls, cenotes (sinkholes), and lush canyons that are an amazing contrast to the high dry deserts just a few hours away.

TEXT-DEPENDENT QUESTIONS

Is the state of Tamaulipas in a hot-weather, medium-weather, or cold-weather area?
What is the name of the river that carved out the Copper Canyon?

RESEARCH PROJECT

Choose one of the northern states of Mexico (Chihuahua, Coahuila, Durango, Nuevo León, San Luis Potosí, Tamaulipas, or Zacatecas) and find out more about its geography. What are the major mountains, rivers, or other natural features within the state? Print out a a map of the state, and label the important geographic features as well as major cities.

CHIHUAHUA

Location: Sonora lies to the west; Coahuila to the east; the United States to the north; and Durango to the south.

Capital: Chihuahua

Total area: 96,364 square miles (247,087 sq km)

Climate: Mostly dry and warm; colder at higher elevations

Terrain: Desert, canyons, some forests at higher elevations

Elevation: High 10,725 feet (3,250 meters) Low 4,921 feet (1,500 meters)

Natural hazards: Drought, earthquakes

COAHUILA

Location: The United States lies to the north; Nuevo León to the east; San Luis Potosí and Zacatecas to the south; and Durango and Chihuahua to the northeast.

Capital: Saltillo

Total area: 58,493 square miles (149,982 sq km)

Climate: Mild, dry

Terrain: Deserts and mountains

Elevation: High 12,172 feet (3,700 meters) Low 2,625 feet (800 meters)

Natural hazards: Earthquakes

DURANGO

Location: Chihuahua and Coahuila lie to the north; Zacatecas to the east; Nayarit to the south; and Sinaloa to the west.

Capital: Durango

Total area: 46,663 square miles (119,648 sq km)

Climate: Moderate with four seasons

Terrain: Mountainous

Elevation: High 10,956 feet (3,320 meters) Low

Natural hazards: Earthquakes

NUEVO LEÓN

Location: Surrounded by Coahuila to the west and north; Tamaulipas to the east; San Luis Potosí and Zacatecas to the south.

Capital: Monterrey

Total area:
25,176 square miles
(64,555 sq km)

Climate: Hot, humid

Terrain: Mountainous

Elevation: High 12,139 feet (3,700 meters) Low 2,953 feet
(900 meters)

Natural hazards:
Earthquakes, mud slides

SAN LUIS POTOSÍ

Location: Coahuila lies to the south, Nuevo León and Tamaulipas to the northeast; Veracruz to the east; Guanajuato, Querétaro, and Hidalgo to the south; and Zacatecas to the west.

Capital: San Luis Potosí

Total area:
24,511 square miles
(62,848 sq km)

Climate: Tropical to cool and arid, depending on altitude.

Terrain: Mountainous

Elevation: High 9,843 feet (3,000 meters) Low 223 feet
(68 meters)

Natural hazards:
Earthquakes

TAMAULIPAS

Location: The United States lies to the north; Veracruz and San Luis Potosí are to the south; the Gulf of Mexico is to the east; and Nuevo León is to the west.

Capital: Ciudad Victoria

Total area: 31,133 square miles (79,829 sq km)

Climate: The north-central part is semi-dry and semi-warm, with scarce rain. The south and southeast parts are warm, with summer rains.

Terrain: Mountainous away from the coast

Elevation: High 9,843 feet (3,000 meters) Low Sea level

Natural hazards: Hurricanes

ZACATECAS

Location: Durango lies to the northwest; Coahuila to the northeast; San Luis Potosí to the east; and Jalisco and Aguascalientes to the south.

Capital: Zacatecas

Total area: 58,654 square miles (150,395 sq km)

Climate: Four types of climate, depending on altitude: semi-warm, dry, mild, and cold.

Terrain: Mountainous

Elevation: High 10,499 feet (3,200 meters) Low 6,594 feet (2,010 meters)

Natural hazards: Earthquakes, volcanoes

 ## WORDS TO UNDERSTAND

aqueduct—a bridge-like above-ground structure that carries water.

cabinet—an advisory council to the head of a government.

cistern—an underground tank where drinking water can be stored.

hacienda—a large Mexican ranch.

immunity—the body's ability to resist certain diseases.

Jesuit—a member of the Roman Catholic Society of Jesus, founded by St. Ignatius Loyola in 1534 and devoted to missionary work.

petition—a formal written request, usually signed by many people.

vaqueros—Mexican cowboys.

This colonial-era aqueduct in Zacatecas, built during the late 18th century, carried water to a place near the city where silver was mined.

THE HISTORY

The stories that have come to us about the history of the northern parts of Mexico are as beautiful and as brutal as the land itself. Long ago, tribes called Chichimecas lived in these desert regions. They could not grow food in land that had no water, nor could they raise livestock. They wandered from place to place, wintering in the warmer parts and spending their summers up higher in the mountains. They would eat whatever they could find—snakes, reptiles, cactus, even insects. In the mountains, they could catch rabbits or gather wild foods.

These Chichimecas—the name given to all of the northern nomads regardless of their tribe—came down from northern Mexico to settle in the central region—the meseta—where the land was fertile and more forgiving. The word "Chichimeca" meant "lineage of the dog," but it was not meant as an insult. Rather, many Aztec dynasties were proud to claim this heritage. But while the Aztecs swept across central Mexico, conquering the other tribes, the people who remained in the north continued to live as they had. Some, such as the Tarahumara or *Rarámuri*, live in this fashion even today.

When the Spanish arrived, conquering the northern part of Mexico took them much longer than they had needed to control the central region of

Mexico. For generations, roving tribes would come down from the mountains, attack the Spanish, and then retreat. The Spanish settlers who were brave enough to venture into northern Mexico were people who planned to stay— miners and ranchers and Catholic priests.

Between A.D. 1000 and 1200, the ancient city of Paquimé thrived in the area that today is the state of Chihuahua. It was the most important trading and farming center in northern Mexico. The people who lived there kept parrots and turkeys in pens; they built *aqueducts* and *cisterns* to supply their city with fresh water. By the time the Spanish came to Mexico, however, the people of Paquimé had disappeared, and the Aztecs had burned their abandoned buildings. Archeologists did not discover the long-ago city until the 1970s.

When the Spanish came to this land, they brought with them horses, cattle, and sheep—and the desert became ranchland that at one time stretched beyond the Río Grande into what is now the United States. The new animals from Europe altered the landscape. It became rangeland, where vast *haciendas* stretched for miles and miles. In Chihuahua, *vaqueros* originated the riding and roping skills we now associate with American cowboys.

The land was secluded and wild, separated from civilization by the desert's sandstorms. During the Mexican Revolution, this seclusion appealed to Pancho Villa, the rebel leader. He established his headquarters in Chihuahua; his band of cowboys and bandits streamed out of the desert to attack the unjust government of Porfirio Díaz—and then they retreated back to the safety of the desert.

COAHUILA

The state of Coahuila is proud of the part it played in Mexican history. Two great leaders of the nation's fight for freedom and equal rights were born in

This mural depicts aspects of ancient Aztec life. Most historians believe that the Aztecs migrated from northern Mexico in the early 13th century.

Saltillo, the state's capital city. The first of these, Francisco Madero, was the first political leader to seize power from Porfirio Díaz, whose harsh rule controlled Mexico for more than 30 years. Madero, a wealthy landowner, challenged Díaz in the elections, and as a result Madero was imprisoned. After his release, Madero fled to the United States, where he called for revolution in Mexico. Under his leadership, the Mexican Revolution was launched, and Díaz was overthrown.

24

Francisco I. Madero (1873–1913) opposed longtime dictator Porfirio Díaz, and was an early leader of the revolution that forced Díaz from power. He served as president of Mexico for two years, until his administration was overthown by a military coup.

The second revolutionary leader to come from Coahuila was Venustiano Carranza. He was a military general who is called the "Father of the Mexican Constitution." He became the governor of his state, and then went on to become the nation's president.

DURANGO

When the Spanish began to settle northern Mexico, their coming nearly destroyed the native people who already lived there. The Spanish turned the Indians into slaves; many of the native people died because they had no *immunities* to the diseases the Spanish brought with them; and the Spanish missionaries tried to take away the Indians' religion and replace it with Christianity.

Revolutionary leader and Mexican president Venustiano Carranza (1859–1920) was born in Coahuila.

But some of the native people fought back. In Durango, between 1616 and 1620, the Tepehuán people fought for their freedom and their rights. The rebellion was led by a man named Quautlatas, who had been flogged by the *Jesuit* missionaries for expressing his doubts about Christianity. Quautlatas encouraged his people to reject Christianity, to recover their faith in their old beliefs, and to drive the Spanish invaders out of their land. He traveled from settlement, fanning the fires of rebellion. He told his listeners that if they were killed in battle against the Spanish, they would be brought back to life seven days after their final victory.

The rebels burned churches and killed more than 400 Spanish settlers and missionaries. The Spanish responded by sending their troops to kill and defeat the Tepehuanes. More than a thousand of the native people were killed, and hundreds more were sold into slavery.

ZACATECAS

Durango was not the only region to experience Indian rebellion. In 1541, Indians in the area that is now Zacatecas burned down the churches and killed the owners of the haciendas. The Spanish swiftly and brutally squashed the uprising, forcing the Indians to flee into the highlands of Zacatecas, a land of steep hills and poisonous scorpions.

After this war, known as the Mixton War, the Spanish felt that they must overpower all the Indians. From Zacatecas, the Spanish moved to conquer the whole area of north-central Mexico. As mines flourished and farms were established, more and more Indians were either made into slaves or forced farther north to less desirable land.

By the 20th century, the mines were running dry, but Zacatecas still had an

Modern view of Zacatecas. In the mid-16th century, a native Amerindian from this region gave a silver trinket to a Spanish colonists and told him the silver had come from the nearby mountains. The small gift sparked a mining rush that would continued for the next 400 years During this period more than a billion dollars worth of silver and other precious metals were stripped from the hills around Zacatecas.

important part to play in Mexican history. The rebel leader Pancho Villa fought an important battle here during the Mexican Revolution, defeating the government's troops.

NUEVO LEÓN

When the Spanish conquered this region they gave it the name of Nuevo Reino de León in honor of Reino de León, an area in Spain. In September 20, 1596, Don Diego de Montemayor, a Spanish conquistador, settled a city here with 12 families. At that time, the city was called La Villa de San Luis de Francia (named for the king of France), but Don Diego later changed the name to Ciudad Metropolitana de Nuestra Señora de Monterrey. Four hundred years later, Monterrey is a modern and industrial city, the third largest in Mexico.

SAN LUIS POTOSÍ

This region was first settled in 1583 as a Franciscan mission, but the community forgot its preoccupation with religion when someone discovered silver in the mountains. Because of the royal fortune beneath the land, it was given a new, royal name in 1592—San Luis, after King Louis IX of France. Potosí was the name of a

The Metropolitan Cathedral of Our Lady of Monterrey rises over the capital of Nuevo León. Construction of the cathedral in Monterrey began in 1635, but it was not completed until 1800. As a result, the building blends a variety of architectural styles, reflecting the diverse influences of northern Mexico's history.

rich Bolivian mining town, and this was tacked on as well, in hopes that this region would prove to be as prosperous as the Bolivian town.

By the 19th century, however, San Luis Potosí had become an out-of-the-way refuge for political liberals who were seeking to escape government persecution. After Napoléon's troops captured Mexico City in 1863, President Juárez brought the remains of his government to San Luis—but then he moved still further north, into Chihuahua.

At the time of the Mexican Revolution, San Luis was still a haven for liberal opposition to the government. Francisco Madero fled here after Díaz arrested him for challenging his presidency. Madero moved on across the border to San Antonio, Texas, but when he drafted his famous plan for a new government, he called it the *Plan de San Luis Potosí*. Madero managed to win his fight against Díaz, but he did not hold the presidency long. By 1913 he had been assassinated, and the revolution splintered in many warring factions.

TAMAULIPAS

During the 1830s, the people of Tamaulipas opposed the central government's rule. They felt that the Mexican government was only plunging them into deeper and deeper economic trouble. They supported a ***petition*** that asked that the president get rid of the existing ***cabinet***, and create an entirely new government.

At the time, Tamaulipas, Coahuila, Nuevo León, and Texas were a single military jurisdiction. Texas eventually achieved its independence from the Mexican government, but Tamaulipas, along with Coahuila and Nuevo León, remained under the Mexican government's repressive control until the Revolution of 1910 brought the entire nation greater freedom.

NORTHERN MEXICO TODAY

The bordern between the United States and Mexico is nearly 2,000 miles long, and it passes through many remote and sparsely populated desert areas. Because of this, it is very challenging for U.S. and Mexican authorities to patrol the long border. Historically, Mexicans seeking greater opportunities have attempted to sneak across the border into the United States from the states of Chihuahua, Coahuila, Nuevo León, and Tamaulipas. In recent decades, smugglers have sought to bring illegal drugs over the border into the U.S.

Drug cartels fight each other for control over smuggling routes. For example, the Gulf Cartel runs smuggling operations around Matamoros, Tamaulipas. Since 2007, the Juárez Cartel and the Sinaloa Cartel have been fighting for control over drug trafficking around Ciudad Juárez.

In 2006, President Felipe Calderón engaged federal soldiers and police to stop the drug cartels. Since then, Mexico has received significant aid from the U.S. government to fight drug smuggling. However, although Calderón's successor, Enrique Peña Nieto, has continued waging the so-called narco conflict, the bloody conflict continues, with more than 120,000 people killed in drug-related violence.

TEXT-DEPENDENT QUESTIONS

In which state did Pancho Villa establish his headquarters during the Mexican Revolution? What is Nuevo León named for?

RESEARCH PROJECT

Using the Internet or your school library, do some research on a famous person from the northern states of Mexico, such as Quautlatas, Don Diego de Montemayor, Francisco Madero, Venustiano Carranza, or Pancho Villa. Write a two-page report about this person's life and present it to the class.

 WORDS TO UNDERSTAND

export—to ship goods or commodities out of an area or country for sale in another country.

import—to bring goods or commodities into a country so they can be sold to consumers in that country.

free trade—the exchange of goods or services between countries that is not subject to governmental restrictions or fees.

A busy street in Ciudad Juárez. which has become a major manufacturing center for Mexico. The city is home to more than 300 small factories, called maquiladoras, which produce a variety of goods that are exported to other countries.

THE ECONOMY

Mexico has a long history of serious economic problems. The gap between the rich and the poor has always been wide and deep, and the government has often done very little to solve the problems of a desperately poor population.

During the administrations of Mexican presidents Vicente Fox (2000-2006) and Felipe Calderón (2006-2012), the government promised to do more to help the poorest people of Mexico. Unfortunately, although their administrations did work to create jobs and to provide services, they ultimately failed to raise the standard of living for millions of Mexicans. In 2014, the average Mexican earned about $12,000 per year. By comparison, the average U.S. resident earned about $44,000 per year.

Poverty is exacerbated by the fact that the huge gap between the rich and poor in Mexico continues to grow wider. According to the Organization for Economic Cooperation and Development (OECD), an international organization of 34 countries (including Mexico and the United States) that was formed to stimulate economic progress and promote world trade, the top 20 percent of Mexico's population earns more than 12 times as much as the bottom 20 percent.

Mexico has the world's 14th-largest economy, with a gross domestic product (the value of all goods and services produced in a year) valued at over $1.3 trillion in 2014. The economy is heavily dependent on **exports**, as Mexico is one of the most receptive countries when it comes to **free trade**. It has signed agreements with many countries, including the United States, China, Japan, the European Union, and many countries of Central and South America. These agreements typically reduce or eliminate trade restrictions and fees on imports and exports, making it less expensive for foreign companies to buy products from Mexican companies.

Of all the free-trade agreements, the North American Free Trade Agreement (NAFTA) is the most important to Mexico's economy. It provides for free trade between the United States, Canada, and Mexico. Since it was signed in 1994, trade between the U.S. and Mexico has increased significantly.

Maquiladoras have created much of the growth. The maquiladoras are assembly plants where the pieces of a product are **imported** into Mexico without any tax. The product is assembled in Mexico. It is then exported from Mexico, again without paying a tax. Most maquiladoras produce products like electronics, textiles, and automobiles. Many of the Maquiladoras are located in the northern states of Mexico, because of their proximity to the U.S.-Mexico border.

Unfortunately, poor working conditions are common in Mexican maquiladoras. The owners of these factories can make their employees work long hours for low pay, and they do not have to obey the sort of safety regulations that are enforced in U.S. factories. This enables them to keep their prices down, which makes them attractive business partners for International companies looking to make as much profit on their products as possible.

A train runs along the Copper Canyon in the Sierra Madre Mountains. The promise of NAFTA has not been fully realized by most Mexicans because the government has failed to upgrade roads and provide infrastructure and technology that could enable greater economic growth.

However, despite the poor working conditions, and even though most of these plants or factories are owned by foreigners, they still boost the economy by providing jobs. This creates the need for more technology. More electricity, running water, housing, roads, and transportation are needed to support all of the people who are working in the *maquiladoras*.

Nuevo León is is one of Mexico's leading industrial areas. It is easy to pass across a new international bridge to the United States, and there are numerous factories that produce iron and steel, glass, textiles, and petrochemicals. Monterrey is the financial center; the city's dozens of *maquiladoras* employ

Silver purses hang for sale at a tourist market. Mexico's folk art is appreciated both inside and outside its borders. Tourism and the souvenir business are thriving.

thousands of workers. Forty percent of the jobs in this state involve manufacturing. In fact, Nuevo León is one of the few places in Mexico where unemployment is not a problem. The government is working to train people to work in the factories because of a shortage of skilled labor.

However, due to the extreme heat and dryness, not much grows in Nuevo León. Cattle raising is the primary agricultural activity.

Good railroads and highways in San Luis Potosí make transporting goods easy. Agriculture and cattle also play an important role in San Luis Potosí's economy. Most of the industry concerns automobiles, mining, food processing, mechanics, textiles, and beverage production. Although San Luis Potosí began as a mining settlement, today most of its economy is built around exporting goods.

The economy of Zacatecas depends mainly on agriculture, livestock, and mining. Main products include guavas, grapes, peaches, and apples. Cattle and sheep graze on more than half the land. Mining of silver, tin, lead, copper, and gold continues. Most of Mexico's silver comes from Zacatecas.

Tarahumara children hoe weeds in a field. Farming is an essential part of Mexico's economy, and NAFTA has opened up international markets for meat and produce grown in the country. However, due to Mexico's poverty many people are reduced to subsistence farming in order to feed their families.

Durango's economic strength is mining and forestry. More than a third of Mexico's timber comes from this state. Wood-related industries make paper, plywood, cross ties, and other wooden items. Most of the industry is located in Ciudad Lerdo and in Gómez Palacio. One third of Durango's economy is based on the farming of crops and livestock.

In Tamaulipas, agriculture is important. Efficient irrigation allows farmers to grow sorghum, wheat, and corn. Fishing along the coast depends upon shrimp, crayfish, oyster, and crabs. Oil production and maquiladoras account for most of the industry. The port of Tampico is one of the most active in the area.

Coahuila gets most of its income from mining and industry. Excellent highways allow goods to be transported easily. Fluorite, lead, and tin mining are important to this state's economy. Foundries take the raw materials and make

Hand-made bricks dry in the yard of a brick factory near Durango. Manufacturing and industry have become key to Mexico's financial future.

steel and iron. Irrigation allows for farming and livestock raising. The area of Laguna is one of Mexico's richest farming regions.

The economy of Chihuahua, Mexico's largest state, largely depends on mining and industry. Most of the manufacturing occurs in maquiladoras along the U.S. border, in the two large cities, Ciudad Juárez and Chihuahua City. Ciudad Juárez remains the major manufacturing area, with about 400 factories in the same town that was at one time a stopping place for cowboys from El Paso. At the beginning of the last century, Chihuahua's economy was more concerned with timber and livestock, but today companies such as Toshiba, JRC, and Honeywell have factories here. In addition, Chihuahua has a number of tourist attractions, including the Copper Canyon.

Although there is no copper in Copper Canyon, the Spanish did find gold and silver as well as turquoise and amethyst there. Today many of the precious metals are gone, but a few prospectors are still trying to make a living there.

The Indians farm along the rivers, primarily raising corn. Almost every family tends to one milpa or cornfield, and there are six types of corn commonly grown here. Other important crops are beans, squash, peaches, apples, and potatoes.

TEXT-DEPENDENT QUESTIONS

What international trade agreement has had an important impact on Mexico's economy? Which of the northern states produces one-third of Mexico's timber?

RESEARCH PROJECT

The North American Free Trade Agreement (NAFTA) is an agreement that eliminates tariffs and other barriers to trade and investment between the United States, Canada, and Mexico. At the time NAFTA was implemented in 1994, many people believed it would improve the standard of living for Mexican workers. Find out more about the agreement and its effect on Mexico's economy, and on the maquiladora system, over the past two decades. Which Mexican industries have benefited from NAFTA, and which have declined as a result of increased competition from foreign companies?

CHIHUAHUA

Gross Domestic Product (GDP):
   $35.5 billion

GDP per capita:
   in pesos: 136,417
   in dollars: $12,338
   rank: 5 of 31

Natural resources: timber, livestock

Economic sectors by percentage of GDP:
   Manufacturing 11%
   Commerce 52%
   Service industries 37%

Exports: minerals, corn, wheat, beans, and meat.

COAHUILA

Gross Domestic Product (GDP):
   $25.7 billion

GDP per capita:
   in pesos: 137,926
   in dollars: $12,474
   rank: 4 of 31

Natural resources: iron ore, lead, silver, zinc, gold, copper.

Economic sectors by percentage of GDP:
   Manufacturing 11%
   Commerce 53%
   Service industries 36%

Exports: iron, cotton, grapes, livestock.

DURANGO

Gross Domestic Product (GDP):
   $10.1 billion

GDP per capita:
   in pesos: 90,000
   in dollars: $8,140
   rank: 14 of 31

Natural resources: timber, mining

Economic sectors by percentage of GDP:
   Manufacturing 13%
   Commerce 53%
   Service industries 34%

Exports: fruit, dairy products, textiles, beans, cotton.

NUEVO LEÓN

Gross Domestic Product (GDP):
   $58.8 billion

GDP per capita:
   in pesos: 180,689
   in dollars: $6,935
   rank: 18 of 31

Natural resources: iron ore, lead, copper.

Economic sectors by percentage of GDP:
   Manufacturing 12%
   Commerce 51%
   Service industries 37%

Exports: glassware, prepared food, iron, beverages and chemicals.

SAN LUIS POTOSÍ

Gross Domestic Product (GDP):
$14.8 billion

GDP per capita:
in pesos: 76,684
in dollars: $6,935
rank: 18 of 31

Natural resources: farmland, gold, silver, lead.

Economic sectors by percentage of GDP:
Manufacturing 12%
Commerce 53%
Service industries 35%

Exports: precious metals, chemicals, fruit.

TAMAULIPAS

Gross Domestic Product (GDP):
$25.2 billion

GDP per capita:
in pesos: 112,785
in dollars: $10,200
rank: 10 of 31

Natural resources: gold, copper, silver, lead, oil, fish and crustaceans.

Economic sectors by percentage of GDP:
Manufacturing 9%
Commerce 51%
Service industries 40%

Exports: petrochemicals, seafood.

ZACATECAS

Gross Domestic Product (GDP):
$5.8 billion

GDP per capita:
in pesos: 56,747
in dollars: $5,132
rank: 26 of 31

Natural resources: gold, copper, silver, lead, zinc, farmland.

Economic sectors by percentage of GDP:
Manufacturing 11%
Commerce 55%
Service industries 34%

Exports: coffee, fruit, fertilizer, sugar, fish and crustaceans.

GDP = Gross Domestic Product, the total value of goods and services produced during the year.

PER CAPITA GDP = the total GDP produced by residents of an area, divided by the total number of people living in that area.

CURRENCY CONVERSION (2014)
1 peso = about 7.5 US cents
1 US dollar = 13.29 pesos

All figures from INEGI, the Mexican National Institute of Statistics, based on Mexico's most recent census.

 WORDS TO UNDERSTAND

fiesta—Spanish party or celebration.

Lent—the six weeks before Easter, a time of fasting and repentance for those who follow the Roman Catholic religion.

mescal—A colorless Mexican liquor distilled from the leaves of maguey plants.

serapes—colorful woolen shawls worn by Mexican men.

Workers construct a modern bridge in Torreón, an industrial center in the state of Coahuila.

THE CULTURE

The northern part of Mexico is much closer to the United States geographically and culturally. Much of what goes on in the towns is directed toward the border—the factories, the tourists who come and go. But outside of the cities, in places like the Sierra Tarahumara, the Indians live as they always have.

There are about 70,000 Tarahumara (or *Rarámuri*) living in the Copper Canyon in caves, under cliffs, and in small cabins. These people raise corn and beans and some animals. The name *Rarámuri* means "running people" or "footrunners," and they are known for how fast they run barefoot up the mountains. They are famous for their nonstop, long-distance foot races that may last as long as 72 hours. The phrase they use to describe their running is "foot throwing." A game they like to play is known as *rarahipa* and involves teams kicking a wooden ball. These people live closely to the earth; they fashion their plows from the limbs of oak trees, and they are skilled in the preparation of more than 200 species of edible plants. They are determined to follow the ancient traditions of their ancestors; for centuries, they have successfully resisted all outside efforts to modernize their way of life.

When you travel from Copper Canyon to a city on the border like Ciudad

12

Juárez, it is almost like traveling through time. The modern border towns have more in common with modern European or American cities than they do with the primitive villages of their own state.

Whether primitive or modern, however, like the rest of Mexico the people of the northern states love to celebrate. They enjoy festivals, fairs, feast days, national holidays, and religious holidays. Every town has its own saint and celebrates on that saint's special day. Local regions also have their own unique celebrations for the harvest of their particular crops. Most of these joyous events involve music, dancing, feasting, and fireworks.

Along with the rest of the nation, northern Mexico celebrates the following holidays:

Carnaval, the Tuesday before the beginning of **Lent**, when people parade through the streets in costumes.

Holy Week, from Palm Sunday to Easter Sunday.

Cinco de Mayo, May 5, when Mexicans celebrate their victory over France at the battle of Puebla in 1862.

Día de la Raza, October 12 (Columbus Day in

	STATE POPULATION	GROWTH RATE
Chihuahua	3,052,907	2.3%
Coahuila	2,298,070	1.6%
Durango	1,448,661	0.7%
Nuevo León	3,834,141	2.2%
San Luis Potosí	2,299,360	1.4%
Tamaulipas	2,753,222	2.1%
Zacatecas	1,353,610	0.6%

Mexico's ethnic groups:
Indian-Spanish (mestizo): 60 percent
Indian: 30 percent
White: 9 percent
Other: 1 percent

Education: 12 years of education is required from ages 6 through 18. About 94 percent of school-age children are enrolled in school. The literacy rate is 91 percent.

Mexico's religions:
Roman Catholic: 77 percent
Protestant: 6 percent
Unspecified response: 17 percent

Two Tarahumara girls use a stick to toss a hoop forward as part of a race. They are participating in games and dances in an effort to keep their traditional culture alive.

43

the United States), when Mexicans celebrate the mingling of races that makes their nation unique.

Día de los Muertos (Day of the Dead), October 31-November 2, when Mexicans honor their dead with celebrations and feasting.

The Feast of the Virgin of Guadalupe, December 12, when Mexicans honor their patron saint.

Advent and Christmas, December 16-25, when Mexicans celebrate *Posada*, honoring Mary and Joseph's search for shelter, and then spend Christmas Day as a quiet religious holiday.

Various local cities and regions have their own celebrations as well.

In Chihuahua, the Tarahumara people have incorporated the festivals of the Virgin of Guadalupe and *Semana Santa* (Holy Week) with their own religious traditions to create the Festival of the Easter Moon. They celebrate these

A poster advertising a bullfight in Monterrey is displayed on a public wall. Many Mexicans are passionate about keeping their culture alive through customs and traditions.

occasions with elaborate costumes and dancing. This festival, held in the springtime, also marks the start of the corn planting season.

From July 18 to August 3, people of Coahuila flood the streets of Saltillo to celebrate the annual *Feria de Saltillo*. This region was first settled by 400 Tlaxcalteca families, people who were craftsmakers and weavers by trade, and Saltillo's fair celebrates their descendants' artistry and culture. Colorful woolen *serapes* are a symbol of these people's traditional lifestyle and unique culture.

Every July, Durango celebrates for two weeks. The festival starts July 4, the day of the *Virgen del Refugio*, and continues through July 22, the anniversary of Durango's founding in 1563. The celebration is known throughout Mexico, and people from all over the country come to buy cows, bet on cockfights, and enjoy the food, music, dancing, and rides.

Monterrey, the capital city of Nuevo León, has a very different annual event—a lottery. Every year thousands of hopeful people buy tickets for the national lottery sponsored by Monterrey's Technology Institute. The grand prize is a dream

Monterrey-born soccer (Fútbol) player Darío Carreño goes for the goal during a game for the professional team Monterrey, CF. This club is the oldest active team from northern Mexico, and has been one of the most successful in recent years. Monterrey, CF won the CONCACAF Champions League, the most prestigious pro tournament in North America, in 2011, 2012, and 2013. The club began playing in a new 50,000-seat stadium in 2014.

house, designed and built by experts chosen by the Institute. The prize also includes enough money to furnish the house—and an additional sum for upkeep for many years to come.

The people of San Luis Potosí celebrate the last two weeks of August. They flock to the capital city for the *Fiesta Nacional Potosina*. The festival includes

46

1993 - 2003
32.0
DONDE ESTAN
LAS MUERTAS
DE JUAREZ?
PARA DARLES
SANTA
SEPULTURA

Celebrations for the Day of the Dead festival may appear morbid to outsiders, but they carry a great deal of significance for Mexican participants.

concerts, bullfights, fireworks, and a parade. The celebration of the city's patron saint, San Luis, also falls during this time.

Come May, the city will again celebrate for another 10 days. This time the *Festival de las Artes* will fill the city with music, dance, and theater performances.

The border towns of Tamaulipas are so close to Texas that the United States is a big influence on their culture. Everything tends to cater to the tourists who come in throngs looking for cheap handicrafts and after-dark thrills in the rough bars and cantinas that fill these cities. This area of Mexico is not famous for its food or drink—but many tourists do enjoy the buzz of caffeine they experience when they drink this region's traditional beverage: *café de olla*, a blend of coffee, chocolate, and cinnamon that is brewed slowly in a clay pot.

The people of Zacatecas sometimes celebrate a private **fiesta** called a *callejonada*. A donkey, with gallons of **mescal** on its back, strolls through the alleys and back streets of the capital city. Music and dancing follow along behind—and everyone is welcome to join the party.

TEXT-DEPENDENT QUESTIONS
Where do the Tarahumara people live? What athletic activity are they known for? What do Mexicans celebrate each year on Día de la Raza, October 12?

RESEARCH PROJECT
The Tarahumara natives of Chihuahua blended the Christian beliefs brought by the Spanish with their own pre-Christian traditions to create their Festival of the Easter Moon. Find out more about this festival, which is celebrated in the springtime and marks the season when the Tarahumara dance, plant corn, and imbibe a special wine called *tesvino*. Write a report describing the events of the festival and present it to the class.

WORDS TO UNDERSTAND

Mennonites—members of a Christian religious group who believe
in pacifism and sometime attempt to isolate themselves
from the influences of modern society.

These homes in Monterrey are built onto the foothills of the Sierra Madre Oriental range. Monterrey, the capital of Nuevo León, is one of the largest cities in Mexico.

CITIES AND COMMUNITIES

Many of Mexico's most modern, wealthy, and industrialized cities lie opposite the United States along the northern border. Some Mexicans feel that the United States dominates Mexico, intruding where it doesn't belong. Many believe that U.S. businesses take advantage of the cheap labor of the Mexican workers.

In these northern cities are the *maquiladoras*—the factories that are often owned by companies from the United States. Here too people regularly go back and forth over the border into the United States, sometimes working in one country and living in the other. Perhaps more than in any other part of Mexico, people in the northern states' cities feel related to the United States. Indeed, they often have relations across the border.

Chihuahua City, with over 825,000 residents, is the 12th-largest city in Mexico and one of its most industrialized. Timber and mining concerns, as well as *maquiladoras*, are based in Chihuahua, although the dog that takes its name from this region is rarely seen here.

Originally settled by silver miners at the start of the 18th century, Chihuahua has served as a refuge for many political figures. Miguel Hidalgo fled here during the War of Independence, and Benito Juárez established Mexico's government here during the French invasion from 1864 to 1867. The city's most famous resident and greatest hero was the outlaw Pancho Villa. In the Museum of the Revolution you can see the car he was driving when he was assassinated in 1923. The car is just as he last saw it, bullet holes and all.

Thanks to NAFTA, Ciudad Juárez (population: 1.3 million) has become an industrial center. Once known as Paso del Norte, Juárez marks the spot where Don Juan de Oñate crossed the Río Grande. This occurred 60 years after the arrival of Cortés and 40 years before the Pilgrims came to Plymouth Rock. In 1668 Father García de San Francisco founded the Mission of Our Lady of Guadalupe, where mass is still said daily. Juárez served as an important way station along the Camino Real (Royal Road), and the cattle drivers would stop here to water their herds on the way to Texas. Some of its most famous inhabitants have included outlaws like Billy the Kid, John Wesley Hardin, and Pancho Villa. In 1856, Benito Juárez established his government here and the city was renamed in his honor.

Unfortunately, the narco conflict that has been waged in Mexico since the mid-2000s has taken a terrible toll on Ciudad Juárez. The city was attractive to drug smugglers due to its proximity to the U.S. border. For many years it was controlled by the notorious drug lord Amado Carrillo Fuentes, known as "Lord of the Skies" because he operated a fleet of jet airplanes that flew drugs into the United States. When Amado died, his brother Vicente took control over what is also known as the Juárez Cartel. In recent years the Carrillo Fuentes organization has been fighting other cartels, most notably the Sinaloa Cartel, for control of drug smuggling in the city. As a result, Ciudad Juárez is considered one of the most dangerous cities in Mexico, with nearly 500 people murdered there in 2014.

A plaza in Durango. The city is located on Mexico's central plateau, at an altitude of 6,170 feet (1,880 m) above sea level.

The state of Chihuahua contains people as diverse as the land itself. In the 1920s, *Mennonite* immigrants from the United States were attracted here by the rich pastures, and today they still maintain their communities in Chihuahua's agricultural areas. Like the Mennonites, the Tarahumara people live in isolation from the rest of the world, but their ancient native culture is far different. The Tarahumara sell their crafts in Chihuahua's cities, and then retreat to their simple lifestyle in Chihuahua's Sierra Madres.

Saltillo, capital of Coahuila, boasts walnut trees, vineyards, and pleasant temperatures. Once a cattle farming town, Saltillo's fresh climate has made it a pleasant stopping place. Saltillo is known for its colorful serapes. The city has a population of about 800,000, making it the 19th-largest municipality in Mexico.

Francisco de Ibarra founded the city of Durango in 1563 and named it after his hometown in Spain. In 1616 Durango was the scene of a bloody Indian rebellion in which 15,000 people died. Today, much of Durango's wealth comes from one of the largest iron deposits in the world, under the mountain Cerro de

52

Mercado. You may have seen the city of Durango a thousand times in the Western movies that were filmed here. Such film stars as John Wayne and Paul Newman have come here to star in Westerns that were filmed in the spectacular desert scenery. The city's current population is about 520,000.

Monterrey, the capital city of Nuevo León, is the ninth-largest city in Mexico with a population of about 1.1 million. Eighty-five percent of Nuevo León's population lives in this modern city. It is a major center of the Mexican steel industry, with numerous steel mills in operation. Many other international conglomerates operate in Monterrey, including Cemex, one of the world's largest cement companies, and Fomento Económico Mexicano (FEMSA), the largest soda bottling company in Latin America. Monterrrey is also known for its many colleges and universities, including the Monterrey Institute of Technology and Higher Education, one of the largest universities in Latin America. Although it is based in Monterrey, the Institute has satellite campuses in Chihuahua, Ciudad Juárez, Saltillo, Tampico, and many other cities in Mexico.

In the 17th century, the city of San Luis Potosí, the state's present-day capital, was the capital of Northern New Spain. It was also home to Juárez, and here he

The Santa Fe bridge across the Río Grande is a major crossing point between Ciudad Juárez and the U.S. city of El Paso, Texas.

This statue of Father Miguel Hidalgo stands in the middle of a village plaza. Following Mexico's Independence Day, this statue will be adorned with red, white, and green flowers to acknowledge Hidalgo's influence in the fight for a free Mexico. The priest-revolutionary was captured and executed by the Spanish in Chihuahua in 1811.

signed the death sentence of the Emperor Maximilian. Today San Luis Potosí calls itself Ciudad de los Jardines, the city of gardens, because of its many parks. Overall, though, this is an industrial city with factories, although the center of the city contains a number of well-preserved old buildings. These led San Luis Potosí to be listed as UNESCO World Heritage Site in 2010. The current population is about 700,000.

Matamoros, directly across the U.S.-Mexico border from Brownsville, Texas, boasts the Museum of Corn as well as a fort left from the Mexican-American War. Matamoros also has a significant Jewish population, because Jewish families from the center of Mexico settled here in the early 20th century to avoid religious persecution. The first *maquiladora* in Mexico was built here, and today there are hundreds of these factories. With about 500,000 residents, Matamoros is the second-largest city in Tamaulipas.

Benito Pablo Juárez was born to Zapotec Indian parents in Oaxaca. He went on to twice be elected president of his country. His desire was to reform the tumultuous government of Mexico.

Nuevo Laredo is located in the state of Tamaulipas on the border of Mexico and the United States. This city was founded in 1755 when Laredo, Texas, became part of the United States. At that time, some Mexican people crossed to the south of the Río Grande to establish a "new" Laredo, because they wanted to remain Mexicans. Between 1950 and 1995, Nuevo Laredo has grown nearly five times over. Currently, it has a population of slightly over 350,000, and it has been projected to grow to over 400,000 residents in the next few years.

Tampico, a bustling port town in Tamaulipas, has a population of 313,400 and is the 44th-largest city in the country. The largest city in Tamaulipas, Tampico was first settled by Huastec Indians and then by the Aztecs. Today, Tampico is still famous for an incident between Mexico and the United States that occurred in 1914. The United States captured the port, helping the rebels overthrow President Huerta.

The city of Zacatecas, the capital of the state, winds like a maze built in between and on top of steep hills. The buildings at the center of town are built from a rosy sandstone, which makes the city seem brightly pink. It was once a prosperous silver town, and it still supplies 34 percent of Mexico's silver. The beautiful Templo de Santo Domingo, filled with ornate golden decoration, was built between 1730 and 1760; it represents of a style of architecture for which Mexico is famous—Churrigueresque. Named for José Churriguera, a Spanish architect, this style is extravagant and fancy; it combined elements of both Spanish and native Mexican architecture.

As you travel from one of these cities to the next, it is impossible not to be struck by the history that lives in each of them. The past and present lie in layers, from modern skyscrapers to ancient churches. The echoes of Nahuatl, Spanish, and English voices come together in an exciting symphony.

Mexico's cities' greatest strength has always come from their people—their unique culture, their creativity, and their faith. The problems handed down from past centuries are still visible in these cities' poverty—but as the Mexican people work with a new administration, who knows how the northern states will grow in the century to come?

TEXT-DEPENDENT QUESTIONS

Which Mexican city was the site of a bloody Amerindian uprising in 1616?

What city in Tamaulipas is directly across the border from Brownsville, Texas?

RESEARCH PROJECT

One of Mexico's most famous contemporary authors, Cristina Rivera Garza, was born in Matamoros in 1964. Using the Internet or your school library, find out more about the author and her works. Write a one-page report and present it to the class.

This ancient pyramid is located at the La Quemada archaeological site, in the state of Zacatecas. The city here was built around A.D. 300 and inhabited until about 1200. Archaeologists believe a small temple or shrine was once located atop the pyramid.

FOR MORE INFORMATION

CHIHUAHUA

Government of Chihuahua
http://www.chihuahua.gob.mx

State Tourism Office
Palacio de Gobierno
Planta Baja
Aldama y Vicente Guerrero
Col. Centro
Chihuahua, Chih.
Tel: (614) 410-10-77
E-mail: cturismo@chihuahua.gob.mx

COAHUILA

Government of Coahuila
http://www.coahuila.gob.mx

State Tourism Office
Av. Universidad
No. 205, Col. Republica Poniente
25280 Saltillo, Coah.
Tel: (844) 416-4880
Fax: (844) 439-2747

DURANGO

Government of Durango
http://www.durango.gob.mx

State Tourism Office
Calle Florida No. 1106, Piso Barrio
El Calvario, Zona Centro
CP 34000
Durango, Dgo.
Tel: (618) 811-2139/1107
Fax: (618) 811-9677
E-mail: turismo@durango.gob.mx

NUEVO LEÓN

Government of Nuevo León
http://www.nuevoleon.gob.mx

State Tourism Office
Antiguo Palacio Federal
Washington ote 648, First Floor
Centro
CP64000 Monterrey, N.L.
Tel: (81) 2020-6789

FOR MORE INFORMATION

SAN LUIS POTOSÍ

Government of San Luis Potosí
http://www.slp.gob.mx

State Tourism Office
Álvaro Obregón No. 520
Zona Central
CP 78000 San Luis Potosí, S.L.P.
Tel: (444) 812-9906
E-mail: turisslp@prodigy.net.mx

TAMAULIPAS

Government of Tamaulipas
http://www.tamaulipas.gob.mx

State Tourism Office
Calle 9 Hernán Cortés No. 136
Col. Pedro Sosa, Edif. El Peñón,
CP 87120 Cd. Victoria, Tamps.
Tel: (834) 315-6248/6249/6136/6137
    ext. 201

ZACATECAS

Government of Zacatecas
http://www.zacatecas.gob.mx

State Tourism Office
Av. Hidalgo No. 403, Segundo Piso
Col. Centro
CP 98000 Zacatecas, Zac.
Tel: (492) 924-0552
Fax: (492) 924-0393

THINGS TO DO AND SEE

CHIHUAHUA
Copper Canyon
Cerocahui's Tarahumar dances and Jesuit mission
Sangre de Cristo gold mines

COAHUILA
La Cascada de Caballo (Horsetail Falls), a dramatic waterfall
Saltillo's cultural center

DURANGO
Regional Museum of Durango, containing fossils and mummies
The city of Durango's Palacio de Gobierno, a baroque palace that houses two of
  Mexico's great 20th-century murals, one by Francisco Montoya and the other
  by Ernesto Flores Esquivel

NUEVO LEÓN
Parque de los Niños Heroes (Park of the Child Heroes), which also contains
  several museums

SAN LUIS POTOSÍ
Santa María del Río, a village famous for its handcrafted silk and cotton shawls.
  These techniques originated in Asia centuries ago, were passed to Spain during
  the Moors' invasion, and then were brought to Mexico by the conquistadors.
Real de Catorce, a ghost town

TAMAULIPAS
The beaches of Tampico
El Cielo Nature Preserve

ZACATECAS
The aqueduct of the city of Zacatecas
Cerro de la Bufa (Hill of the Wineskin), a hill that allows a magnificent view of
  the surrounding landscape; a museum, chapel, and cemetery are also on the hill
Eden Mine, which operated from the 1500s until 1964

Further Reading

Berdan, Frances F. *Aztec Archaeology and Ethnohistory*. London: Cambridge University Press, 2014.

Coe, Michael D., and Rex Koontz. *Mexico: From the Olmecs to the Aztecs*. New York: Thames and Hudson, 2008.

Gritzner, Charles F. *Mexico*. New York: Chelsea House, 2012.

Kent, Deborah. *Mexico*. New York: Children's Press, 2012.

Levy, Daniel C., and Kathleen Bruhn. *Mexico: The Struggle for Democratic Development*. Berkeley: University of California Press, 2006.

Simon, Suzanne. *Sustaining the Borderlands in the Age of NAFTA: Development, Politics, and Participation on the US-Mexico Border*. Nashville: Vanderbilt University Press, 2014.

Internet Resources

Mesoweb
http://www.mesoweb.com/welcome.html#externalresources

National Geographic
http://kids.nationalgeographic.com/kids/places/find/mexico

CIA World Factbook
https://www.cia.gov/library/publications/the-world-factbook/geos/mx.html

History of Mexico
http://www.history.com/topics/mexico

SERIES GLOSSARY

adobe—a building material made of mud and straw.

Amerindian—a term for the indigenous peoples of North and South America before the arrival of Europeans in the late 15th century.

conquistador—any one of the Spanish leaders of the conquest of the Americas in the 1500s.

criollo—a resident of New Spain who was born in North America to parents of Spanish ancestry. In the social order of New Spain, criollos ranked above mestizos.

fiesta—a Mexican party or celebration.

haciendas—large Mexican ranches.

maquiladoras—factories created to attract foreign business to Mexico by allowing them to do business cheaply.

mariachi—a Mexican street band that performs a distinctive type of music utilizing guitars, violins, and trumpets.

Mesoamerica—the region of southern North America that was inhabited before the arrival of the Spaniards.

mestizo—a person of mixed Amerindian and European (typically Spanish) descent.

Nahuatl—the ancient language spoken by the Aztecs; still spoken by many modern Mexicans.

New Spain—name for the Spanish colony that included modern-day Mexico. This vast area of North America was conquered by Spain in the 1500s and ruled by the Spanish until 1821.

plaza—the central open square at the center of Spanish cities in Mexico.

pre-Columbian—referring to a time before the 1490s, when Christopher Columbus landed in the Americas.

INDEX

63

PICTURE CREDITS

ABOUT THE AUTHOR

Deirdre Day-MacLeod is a freelance writer. She lives in Montclair, New Jersey. She is also the author of *Mexico's Central States*.